D0931783

4880 Lower Valley Road, Atglen, Pennsylvania 19310

A large, door-high Art Deco mask of blackened ceramics for a (perhaps too) small fire opening. Design: Gio Ponti.

Holger Reiners

FIREPLACES

Modern Designs—Traditional Forms

Schiffer Publishing Ltd

4880 Lower Valley Road, Atglen, Pennsylvania 19310

The open fireplace as a room installation.
Variously colored marble plates form a
diamond design over the open fireplace.

photo on page 1:
A fascinatingly simple fireplace mask of marble plates with an inlaid decorative element
that directs the view to the center of the fireplace. Architects: H. Pfeiffer & Ch. Ellerman

Other Schiffer Books on Related Subjects
The Fireplace Design Sourcebook. Melissa Cardona. ISBN: 0764322834. $24.95
Fire Spaces: Design Inspirations for Fireplaces and Stoves. Tina Skinner. ISBN: 076431694X.
  $34.95

Copyright © 2010 by Schiffer Publishing
Library of Congress Control Number: 2010923534

Book originally published by Callwey as KAMINE: Aktuelle Entwürfe-Traditionelle Formen.

Designed by Mark David Bowyer
Type set in Humanist 521 BT

ISBN: 978-0-7643-3490-0
Printed in China

Schiffer Books are available at special discounts for bulk purchases for sales promotions
or premiums. Special editions, including personalized covers, corporate imprints, and
excerpts can be created in large quantities for special needs. For more information contact
the publisher:

Published by Schiffer Publishing Ltd.
4880 Lower Valley Road
Atglen, PA 19310
Phone: (610) 593-1777; Fax: (610) 593-2002
E-mail: Info@schifferbooks.com

For the largest selection of fine reference books on this and related subjects,
please visit our web site at **www.schifferbooks.com**
We are always looking for people to write books on new and related subjects.
If you have an idea for a book please contact us at the above address.

This book may be purchased from the publisher.
Include $5.00 for shipping.
Please try your bookstore first.
You may write for a free catalog.

In Europe, Schiffer books are distributed by
Bushwood Books
6 Marksbury Ave.
Kew Gardens
Surrey TW9 4JF England
Phone: 44 (0) 20 8392 8585; Fax: 44 (0) 20 8392 9876
E-mail: info@bushwoodbooks.co.uk
Website: www.bushwoodbooks.co.uk

CONTENTS

FIREPLACE FASCINATION

MODERN DESIGNS— TRADITIONAL FORMS

Today we heat our apartments and houses with almost invisible and inaudible technology – and yet we yearn for the open, direct fire in the fireplace. If it were the only source of warmth in the cold season, our comfort and well-being would have to suffer much. The practical, useful value of a fireplace as an exclusive source of heat and a place to cook belongs to history, but a burning fire also gives us a special kind of comfort, even today: The calming and absorbing view of the dancing flames during an intense conversations by the fire creates an atmosphere from which even statesmen and their work profit when, after long, laborious negotiations, the agreeable solution is often found beside the fireplace.

Ignored, torn down or scorned as not modern, the fireplace has for many years been missing from our functional and factual outlook on living architecture. But not in other lands—Britain, France, and America—fortunately. Here a tradition of fireplace enthusiasts has lived on, continued by modern means and leading, here too, to a renaissance of fireplace building and its cultivated—and also energy-saving—utility.

This book presents an impressive gathering of over 150 fireplaces in all styles, which are useful and attainable again today. Simple fireplaces, fantastically unusual examples, classically modern forms, rustic fireplaces, costly antiquities, and even replicas of historic and antique fireplace frames, all demonstrate the manifold possibilities and wealth of creative designs from past centuries to the present day. With an inclusive chapter on new, modern architectural designs it is shown what independent formative expressions are being found for building fireplaces, and what fascination can arise from it, just as from the artistic forms of old.

Whoever wants a fireplace for the house should inform him- or herself on numerous matters: technical aspects that will determine a fireplace's later, trouble-free function must be planned carefully. Therefore, the necessary facts about the functional and legal aspects of fireplace planning, the design and the choice of materials, as well as the building procedure are handled—without the benefit of a construction manual or a textbook, but rather as a stimulus for one's own planning, as a wealth of ideas and bases for discussion with the planning architect or fireplace builder.

This book should be an inspiration for those builders who would like to install a fireplace in their own house or apartment, and a visual delight for anyone who is interested in the long, fascinating tradition of fireplace design.

A classical Art Deco motif of colored marble plates. The stepped plates lead the eye toward the fire.

Fireplace Fascination | 9

NEW ARCHITECTURAL DESIGNS

Fireplace design is not a new design task of our time. There are examples with a tradition reaching back across centuries that have set certain criteria. Big names in architecture have written fireplace history—into the twenties and thirties. Art Deco was the last tangible epoch in which the fireplace, the fireplace screen, and the fireplace room have experienced a real evaluation as a total work of art and an independent design task. Present-day builders relate to that period when they entrust to their architects or designers the task of designing a fireplace—and maybe even a fireplace room. Every epoch has its own stylistic means of expression; a design should be timely and seek formal answers to the expectations of our time. Thus it is good that architects, after many decades of design abstinence, are taking up this task again today, and that scarcely any of them can escape the fireplace's fascination. Thus builders are encouraged to entrust an architect with this charming and expressive task. The illustrated designs show what a broad spectrum the fireplace offers as a challenge to the designer.

Imaginative shapes, unusual proportions, materials and combinations of materials, artistic paintings, collages and space-seizing designs, and even completely independent works of art frame the fire, independent of whether the fireplace is to function as an open type or a source of heat. All these designs portray unique designs; they are based on the available space and defined by their formative intention.

The uniqueness of the spatial location enhances a fireplace's charm, as does an understanding of how to artfully use fire. The fireplace is now an optional component of living, not a necessary one. The designs reflect this as well. The fascination with the materials is tangible, the intended effect of the chosen proportions, the creation of fireplaces that seem to belong to the past. The fireplace is becoming as lively in present-day life as it was many centuries ago. The open fire symbolizes archaic worlds as well as present-day longings. Finding a functional solution for the available space that meshes with the owner's individual concepts is, and will remain, a fascinating designing task. Whoever does not value classic fireplace frames and does not want to mess around with antiquities, but rather seeks a modern-day answer to his very personal tastes and longings, should inspire an architect to undertake this task. Uniqueness as a result of such an undertaking will reward this individual in a special way—and thus perhaps write fireplace history again one day.

A wall-high fireplace mask of etched glass and brushed stainless steel for the frame and baseplate.
Architects: Gatermann + Schossig.

A wall-dominating fireplace mask of stepped marble plates, which stand out as they shorten the room's depth perspective and direct the eye into the depths. Architect: Wolfgang Doering

The three-dimensional fireplace: The marble of the floor continues in the fireplace frame.
The flue and smokestack are made of polished stainless steel.
Architect: Ulrich Coersmeier.

Two strong marble plates serve as segments of the fireplace ledge and the access to the fire box. The actual fireplace mask is a polished surface that is framed by a walled union of concrete slabs.
Architect: Berthold Rosewich

An axially emphasized fireplace design in which the chimney's length extends over both living levels. The fireplace mask of marble is enclosed with stainless steel, as is the convection slit.

Left: A wall-high fireplace block of
concrete with attached marble plates,
which continue as floor panels.

A classically strict fireplace design with a mask of French limestone.
The gentle forward and backward steps of the plates gives the fireplace
structure a special plasticity.
Design: Franz C. Demblin.

A decorative black fireplace block with a stainless steel smokestack and front. Decorative and functional elements are the stylized fire grate and irons, their spheres forming a successful contrast to the severity of the fireplace block.

Natural stone fireplace wall with a rough frame and sidepieces. The wood storage areas are located to the right and left. The marble covering is continued in the hearth extension over the floor. The fireplace as an important formal element of the integrated spatial concept.
Architect: Rouli Lecatsa, Hamburg.

A heating fireplace with a natural stone frame and spark protector (hearth extension). The lower air intake openings and the upper warm air outlets find their formal expression in the square natural wood fields. The voluminous wood storage areas indicate the actual heating function of the fireplace. Architect: Mai Zill Kusen.

Left: Wall construction includes natural stone plates and stainless steel profiles. Architect: Mai Zill Kusen.

A heating fireplace with lower air intakes and upper air outlets. The burning takes place behind glass, but the fireplace can also be used when opened. Architect: Mai Zill Kusen.

Right: The clear design of this open fireplace succeeds through the functional arrangement of the individual building elements: The marble supports the hearth, the steel hood forms the flue, and the polished mirror conceals the course of the chimney.

A space-saving solution for a heating fireplace. Like a picture frame, the natural stone frames the hearth. The openings for the air circulation are below. The extending natural stone plate is both spark protector and a decorative place to store wood.
Architects: AGN, Bernhard Busch.

Right: Two-tone ceramic heating fireplace with external chimney column. Scholl Ceramics.

Below: The fireplace as a three-dimensional space as well as an original open hearth.
Architect: Rolf Leinweber.

A fireplace made of cast concrete components—
a deliberately angular counterpoint to the
rounded form of the roof.
Architect: Ingrid Spengler, Hamburg.

Lower left: Here the strong concrete mantle of
the hearth has a protective function and is likewise a radiating body, which provides pleasantly
even warming of the area.

The central extension and the decorative holes in the concrete indicate the
production process of this fireplace,
made of two pre-cast parts. The iron
cover conceals the flue; the smokestack
is finished in high gloss paint.

The formation can scarcely be simpler—but what an effect! Few elements, the slim base growing out of the wall, the colored frame that continues as the base border, and the bricks of the hearth for a striking, purist unity.

Left: Like a folded wall screen, the sharply angled, polished stone wings lead the eye to the hearth with effective dramaturgy. The large, polished steel plate is a spark protector as well as a decorative element.
Design: Peter Preller

The fireplace in the open kitchen is a decorative attention-getter as well as a work area.
Near the fireplace is the door of the baking oven, which is heated from the back.

This hot-air fireplace fulfills several functions: it heats, can be used as an open fireplace, and serves as a room divider.
The blackened metal depends in form on the shape of the lower carrier.
Architects: Storch + Ehlers.

Even if it does not burn and is perhaps not even intended for a real
fire, the fireplace is still an effective
symbol of comfort in the spatial and
visual axis.

Left: The fireplace looks as if it were
stamped out of the wall, with its accurate
wall connection in striking contrast to the
fireplace wall and the traces of soot.

Glazed concrete forms the mantle of the
fireplace; its heating unit can be closed
by a cleanly detailed double glass door.
The air intakes and outlets were located
out of sight on the sides.

The right proportions turn this simple fireplace with a steel frame into a convincing interior-architectural element. The double-walled design of the fireplace block is conceived as an effective additional room heater. The hearth lies at floor level, the ash pit is sunken. For better heating effect, the hearth can be closed off by lowering panels. Architects: De Biasio + Scherrer.

The simple, large-surface fireplace formation affords an interesting formative contrast through the inlaid marble plate in the floor. The right and left air intake flaps are also symmetrically arranged.
Architect: Werner Girsberger.

A striking entrance that prepares one for a special impression of space, its axiality and symmetry being especially emphasized by the location of the fireplace.
The covering of the fireplace is a three-centimeter Nero Assoluto plate.
Architects: D. Schnebli—T. Ammann—F. Ruchat-Roncati.

A classically simple fireplace frame with a slightly protruding mirror above it. The inset ash drawer under the hearth makes cleaning easier.
Architects: GPF Guenter Pfeifer.

The artistic formation of the fireplace wall responds to the clear, construction-emphasized architectural expression of the house, with its colored panels seeming to suggest furniture. Architect: Berthold Rosewich; Sculptor: Jakob Broder.

Right: On the same floor of the house, in the master bedroom, is a second fireplace. It was also formed in cooperation with the artist: restful colored pillows frame the hearth, which relates to the total wall of the room in an interesting formal space of excitement.
Architect: Berthold Rosewich; Sculptor: Jakob Broder.

Like a faceted stone, the polished steel frame
surrounds the painted fireplace wall with the
suggestion of a cornice that can be illuminated
decoratively from above. The shelf above the
steel frame can be hung with a spark protector.

This fireplace wall creates the mood of a large oven shape from the days of revolutionary architecture—it acts as both room divider and art form.

The fireplace as an architectural center, toward which everything is directed; even the small colored squares in the wall help to center the room on the fireplace.

An interesting combination of an imaginative old mask and a simple brick fireplace block. The imposing wood storage area indicates active use.

Right: It can scarcely be more reduced: Sheet iron, wall-high, cut out, and angled—a convincingly purist formation, and yet a powerful effect.

A bowed sheet of steel forms the body of the fireplace and the adjacent wood storage.

The body of the fireplace is set on a strong marble plate that also serves as a spark protector.

Right: The theme of this combined open fireplace with adjacent tile oven is the open hearth, which was formed here as an object to be walked around in the middle of the room. Architect: Gert M. Mayr-Keber.

Like the steps of a temple, the
fireplace "walks into" the room.
Stainless steel forms the fire pit
and flue, as well as the spark
protector on the floor.
Architect: Berthold Rosewich.

This air-circulation fireplace
flush with the wall is covered by
a cutout, sandblasted raw iron
plate, behind which the warm air
outlets and air intakes are hidden.
A raw iron plate also serves as a
spark protector, which is set into
the parquet floor.
Architects: De Biasio & Scherrer.

The fireplace as a room divider with the half-open kitchen
immediately creates a pleasant mood full of associations.

Left: As a pleasant half-cylinder, this air circulation fireplace is part of a wall formation that expresses light and fire. Architect: Hans Haeusler.

A small ceramic heating fireplace is an eye-catcher in the stairwell. Scholl Ceramics.

Though not in the center, the fireplace functions as a decorative open fire that attracts the eye to the rough wall. The covering is made of sheet steel, painted with anthracite-colored iron glitter. Architect: AGN, Bernhard Busch.

Exciting crackling: The fire under glass can be observed until the smoke enters the chimney. Boley.

Steel is the dominant material in this interior architecture, with the fireplace as an island of coziness.
Architect: Heinz Peter.

Right: In this open design, the fireplace is the optical center, imaginary wall, seating – and room sculpture with a dominant effect.
Architect: Rolf Leinweber.

Set into the wall, this open fireplace serves as an eye-catching, attention-grabbing phenomenon, or—with a deflected look—a cozy background decoration. Architect: Hans H. Seibold; design and interior architecture: Peter Preller.

Right: An almost ritual formation of the fireplace landscape, whose formal message is longing for relaxed togetherness.

FANTASTIC FIREPLACES

The fireplace as an artisan's experimental field: creating an artistic room sculpture, a picture carrier, and a sculptured fireplace simultaneously. These imaginatively formed fireplaces break with convention. Traditional fireplace structures and inclusions become alienated, caricatured, or want to be understood as independent works of art. The fireplace is in any case a singular furnishing element, so why not design it as such, emphasize and even overvalue it? Didn't the freestanding faience stoves, imaginatively formed iron heating sculptures, and splendid tile ovens have a similar appeal? They too were more than merely functional heating devices. As unconventional as the fantastic new fireplaces are, yet they stand out as independent artistic works in a centuries-long tradition. The once-common practice among art-sensitive builders and buyers of entrusting an artist with the design of the fireplace, or decorating parts of the fireplace structure with a work of art, finds its followers in these formations. To form the fireplace masks and three-dimensional bodies out of a hearth and flue, almost any materials from which relief and sculptures can be formed are suitable. Ceramic tiles or hollow bodies, permanently burned, are combined to form a heating fireplace; plaster, cement or concrete structures are shaped three-dimensionally or painted. Material collages that symbolize the theme of fire and flame are built, or completely free artistic forms are invented—scarcely any limits are set to the fantasy of fireplace formation. They are *objets d'art* that invite one to use them and thus have a utilitarian value above and beyond their static "only being art." In addition to a high elegance that makes many of these fireplaces appear so dominant and space filling, they are challenging designs that require a courageous builder. Any customer who deals with tradition so imaginatively will, under the right circumstances, also have the courage to separate himself from the space filling object some day. Thus, the fireplace formation will take on the burden of unique and eternal expression. This creates the room for independent creativity.

The fire is merely the initial reason for this three-dimensional fireplace that stretches across a whole wall, made of colored cement and variously worked steel.

A combination of individual copper plates serves as an artistic canvas for this fireplace block, created as art with the fire as its ritual center.

With an axial view, the fireplace with its open fire dominates the scene. Viewed from the side, the bar develops behind the fireplace, forming a desirable, functional island.

Upper left: The table seems to have been cut out of the wall. Behind it, the open fire in the fireplace is hidden in the pyramidal treasure chamber.

Ceramic fragments derived from Antonio Gaudis' architecture imaginatively clothe the fireplace mantel.

Lower left: A temple of its own for the fire, its costly materials symbolizing the significance of the fire. Architect: Wolfgang Knoll.

Right: A small ceramic temple for the heating fireplace. Wodtke.

Below: A post-modern arch of triumph for the fire.

Large geometric forms stand as deputies of the elements in this dramatic fireplace conception.

New forms for the ceramic fireplace: From the typical fireplace to the individual solution, this stove-builder's handiwork again offers a broad palette of varied fireplace types. Scholl Ceramics.

Folkloristic patterns formed of tiles and plates—the ideal materials for whoever wants to design his fireplace mantel himself.

Decorative industrial sheet steel forms the frame and spark protector for this unusual fireplace.

The stylized flame of polished steel and sheet brass—also dynamic flaring-up when the flames are not burning on the marble hearth.
Interior Architect: Michael Dressler

Left and right: Two ovens in one house: The mighty fireplace oven—that can also operate with an open door—heats two stories. Its massive form is de-emphasized by the lively artistic workmanship. At the same time, the lively colors banish any association with coldness and the need to supply heat. In the upper story, the tile-oven wall with the warm air outlets and radiation surface forms a meditative wall screen, in whose stream of hot air thoughts translated into shapes seem to swing. Architect: Sinja Gasparin; Artistic formation: Barbara Plecko-Putz.

RUSTIC FIREPLACES

Even though the plastics industry has meanwhile attained remarkable results in producing strong but feather-light "worm-eaten" beams, it has thus contributed to bringing an independent, unmistakable building style into disrepute: the rustic. The rural simplicity, the robust, uncomplicated structures that primarily has a utilitarian function to fulfill, takes on its charm from its sparing use of material and limited working of the individual parts, which are then economically combined and form a functioning, useful utensil. Its beauty is often in this original economy, which indicates that any further work to refine it is unnecessary. The rustic is fascinating because its concise styling means is a universal, an easily understood artisan language with the message:

Here the form follows function alone, the materials are easy to obtain and work, and their functional blend reveals a tradition of handcrafting of techniques that have been used for centuries. Part of being rustic is that to this day utensils or architectural elements are made by the same simple, unchanging rules, that they are durable, with signs of use being part of their special formative charm. The rustic does not necessarily have to be old, but it must be able to become old, its charm is in its natural patina, its "design" feature is the secret anonymity of its artisan—and not a deliberate clumsiness or the false comfort of imitated old beams.

The classic décor of the rustic fireplace is the material in its original form. The formation takes place in a traditionally intuitive manner at the building site, and minor unevenness is accepted as part of the bargain for the sake of the total impression.

In order to preserve the original large fireplace's powerful effect, a smaller flue was installed in the same material—and the illusion is perfect.

The essence of a fireplace that unites all the rustic elements: simple materials and forms as symbols of a deliberately archaic means of construction.

Only the stylistic signs of the simple materials and forms still indicate that this fireplace once belonged in a rural environment. And yet its effect is unusual and impressive.

Simple veined boards and a simple mantel create a somewhat rough but homelike environment for the fireplace.

The proven building materials for the chimney are used creatively to become a dynamic motif of flames.
Sometimes it is good to leave out a few bricks…

Here the cabinetmaker has cooperated and machined the profiles of the fireplace frame. And yet the simple rural character is retained.

REPLICAS OF CLASSIC FIREPLACE FRAMES

In an era of perfect copies and the deceptively exact recreation of works of art and furniture, the replication of classic fireplace frames has maintained its own place in artistic handicrafts. It does not want to be more than a replication, does not want to imitate age, and has no wish to be an antiquity. The replica rather goes back to proven forms and styles and makes use of the materials that were traditionally used by experienced handcrafters in the various epochs of building history, often for generations in exactly the same form or with slight variations. These handcrafted "originals" have written fireplace history over the centuries; one still finds them today in many old houses in England, France, and newer examples in Germany as well. The only function of these artistically handcrafted, often expertly built fireplace frames is decoration. They are the decorative frames for the fire, and they recall epochs in building history in which the fireplace frame was an indispensable accessory of any artistic interior décor. Equally refined were the decors of these frames. Most finely tuned to the proportions of the individual elements and the decorative details, they were in deliberate formal competition with the actual purpose of the fireplace, the fire. Thus these fireplaces were also charming when the fire was not burning. Wall formation, fireplace framing, and hearth, often especially decoratively enclosed, formed a harmonious unity which often, highlighted by a wall-high mirror or a painting over the fireplace, became a special interior-architectural center. The present-day producers of replicas refer back to this heyday of large-scale fireplace formation. They continue a handcrafting and stylistic tradition, make use of traditional materials such as natural stone, wood, and stucco, and create decorative elements with which interiors can be created in the classic styles from Baroque to early Second Reich. Replicas of wood and natural stone live through their effect, from their décor and materials. This is true of the natural stone worked by artisans, just as of the carpentry work of wooden fireplace frames. Stucco, on the other hand, can be applied, according to its stylistic period, either in its fine structure as a white original material or also colored, decoratively patinaed or fixed. In a replica, the handcrafting work of the creation stands in the foreground, not the deceptive impression of a copy intended to attain perfection. Like the original, the replica can also age and take on a patina over time. It is the most economical alternative to real antiquity.

A striking counterpoint to a painted wall and a sandstone fireplace frame is formed by this replica of a slightly exotic, classic English fireplace surround.

The five wooden replicas are a small selection of the fireplace surrounds made by a specialist firm in England with motifs from the period around 1760. The fire grates are also replicas. Hallidays Antiques.

Stepping back into the eighteenth century:
Fireplace surrounds and wall paneling from England,
made with handcrafting perfection and absolute
fidelity to style—for those who like them—are
the incarnation of the cultivated fireplace room.
Hallidays Antiques (see also page 83).

These traditional Baroque and pseudo-classic fireplace surrounds are impressively made handcrafted replicas and can be used as historical eye-catchers or as parts of a whole fireplace formation typical of its time. Leonardo Caminetti.

Through the installation of flue shortenings and oven plates, the hearth opening can be changed without destroying the proportions of the fireplace masks. Oven plates with motifs from the applicable style epoch and in fitting dimensions can even increase the effect of the fireplace. Leonardo Caminetti.

With this fireplace mask, profiled like a marble picture frame, other styling directions and materials in the room are nicely harmonized. Leonardo Caminetti.

The fireplace as a costly eye-catcher with a marble mask, brass inset for the flue, and artistically created replica andirons. Leonardo Caminetti.

Historical fireplace masks made of stucco offer an interesting material variation from wooden fireplace frames. They are noticed both for the perfection of their casting technique and their porcelain-like material effect. Johann Tuemmers.

Styled fireplace masks can be
expanded by a great many drawn
or cast stucco profiles into
complete interior decorations—
either in classic white or colored
form. Johann Tuemmers.

ANTIQUITIES

In the Romance and Anglo-Saxon lands, splendid fireplaces have been indispensable optical focal points of any refined room formation for centuries. Interior architectural composition of plating, appliqués, mirrors, and girandoles create a formally artistic drama, so as to satisfy the observer's eye with a firework of decoration: The fireplace becomes the excuse for well-made architectural fantasies and a triumphant sign that the power of the fire is tamed. From this position, genuine works of art have arisen, to be offered on the present-day antique market as desirable collectors' items. Such precious gems are found mainly in England, France, and Italy, where clever dealers from all over Europe are constantly searching for houses being demolished, for castles or once-elegant country houses, in order to rescue the costly fireplace masks, or even whole interiors, from destruction. Removed and transferred, they then come on the market as desirable antiquities. It is noticeable in these old pieces that they transport us into a different, earlier time, which in hindsight represents a desired, especially glittering, and cultivated form of living and interior decoration. Fireplace frames from the time between about 1600 and the end of the nineteenth century are usually examples of artistic handcraft, expensively made, with costly materials, inlays of stone and wood, gildings, and bronze applications with classic ram- or bullheads decorating the fireplace masks. Or they are complete architectural structures that were designed around the fire pit, with columns, gables, and pillars, supported by caryatids, busts, and sphinxes, eagles, lions, and winged victories stand guard beside the fireplace opening—symbols of power, not only over fire. Eclecticism allows all epochs to appear again in fireplace masks, blending their original styling features with any given transition, so that one might experience in Art Nouveau a flowering of fireplace formation, in which many well-known artists were involved around 1900.

The preferred materials at that time were bronze, chased brass, cast iron, and wood, as well as faience, which are ideally suited for creating floral motifs. The end of its own formative culture around the fireplace was subsequently embodied in Art Deco, which with its strict forms and a wistful remnant of subtle design and perfect craftsmanship leads on to the Modern style. In the end, it lost sight of the fireplace as an object and an architectural beacon for decades. Thus, for the lover of antiquities, the fireplace mask from an especially treasured architectural epoch is now a rewarding constructive finishing touch to suitable furniture and furnishings, or it may also serve as an interior architectural accent. Such antique fireplace masks are imbued with a very specific aura; they create spiritual links with another time, another country, and an often-refined cultural understanding, all the while echoing an earlier courtly ambience. Costly historical fireplace frames require their own architectural framework.

A splendid original fireplace from the region around Macon, France, made around 1900. The sandstone front was cleverly united inside with stone of the same color, reduced to the necessary size for the flue and chimney. Michaele Ferk.

This original (limestone) fireplace frame from the eighteenth century was built up with old bricks and sandstone plates from its time. Since no signs of use can be seen, the fireplace is probably meant only for decoration. Th. Evers.

Right: A reset early sandstone fireplace from France (eighteenth century), with new natural stone frontal area and reflective stonework—such a fireplace is not meant for new houses with small rooms. Th. Evers.

An impressive English fireplace frame from 1790, the great era of pseudo-classic fireplace formation—made of white marble with Verde antique inlays. The Antique Fireplace Warehouse.

An artistic work of sculpture from England at the beginning of the nineteenth century.
The basic form is made of white Carrara with inlays of Siena marble. The Antique
Fireplace Warehouse.

An American fireplace frame
from the nineteenth century
built up and brought to the
functionally right format with
old stones. It includes the
entire wall as a mirror and
frame.

An original fireplace frame in Louis XVI style, with griotte marble intarsia—a simple form that charms with its combination of materials. Michaele Ferk.

A fireplace mask from France, built around 1745, joins with other antiques to become a collection ensemble of the eighteenth century. Michaele Ferk.

An original fireplace front from France, circa 1790, with contemporary andirons.
The mirror frame over the fireplace was finished as a stucco profile. Michaele Ferk.

A fireplace front from France, circa 1880, in Louis XVI style, with original bronze ornamentation. A simple, convincing form that can be combined well with modern furnishings. Michaele Ferk.

A French copy, circa 1880, of a fireplace from the time of Louis XV, of Carrara marble with new angled marble insets and brick walls. Michaele Ferk.

An antique fireplace front—here an original French fireplace from the eighteenth century—is a costly antique of fascinating handcrafted quality. Oellers Imex.

Artistic handcrafted element of an original French fireplace from the eighteenth century, of significant visual and tangible charm. Oellers Imex

A Belgian copy from 1880 of an Empire fireplace, effective through its clear architectural structure and combining well with modern interiors. Th. Evers.

A lovely original classic fireplace of the nineteenth century, especially charming through the lively structure of the material. The stones of the brickwork, some with burned colors, need only the soot traces of use to be able to develop their lovely patina. Oellers Imex.

An old American fireplace front, circa 1830, with a new marble plate that makes the hearth opening smaller. Despite their space-seizing size, these wall-defined masks always retain an intimate character.

Left: An interesting filigreed French original frame from the eighteenth century; its unusual proportions require a good chimney. The old stones of the brickwork, that emphasize the flames, are also noteworthy. W. Schmerhorn.

A rare example of an Art Deco fireplace, with half-round columns that seem to embrace the fire. W. Schmerhorn.

FIREPLACE OVENS

The fireplace oven blends the charm of the open fire with the three-dimensional appeal of the traditional stove that stands free from the wall. In technically refined models, the heat production is so good that the fireplace oven can replace central heating in the spring and fall and efficiently enhance it in the winter. The high-performance heating system, to be sure, is located behind the closed oven doors. But whoever wants to enjoy the play of the flames and the crackling of the fire can also open the doors at times, whereupon such a fireplace oven must be attached to its own chimney connection. Along with the advantages of the either opened or closed operation, the fireplace oven offers a reasonably priced alternative to the open hearth, for it can be installed within a few hours—quickly fulfilling the desire for one's own fireplace. As interesting as the low price of simple models is, it can be so alluring to see the fireplace oven as a high-value, decorative element of home furnishing, which of course has scarcely any upper limits in terms of price either. Readily available fireplace ovens are made of cast iron and ceramics in modern and historical forms. Old and antique ovens with new heating units made of iron, or faience and tile ovens, are rare in good quality and thus have the prices of artistic collectors' items. Such old stoves can usually be

An antique: an original fireplace oven from the nineteenth century, which can also be used with open doors as an open fireplace. Antiquitaeten Mylin.

dismantled, which makes them easier to transport and later allows them to be revised as antiquities. Good pieces can be sought or offered for sale directly in the trade, at auctions or in classified ads. The alternatives to originals and replicas for the fan are individual handcrafted ovens created by present-day designers and made in small series, usually built of steel or iron, or as ceramic stoves that are produced as individual pieces with artistically designed tiles.

All in all, the fireplace oven, as an artistic handcrafted utilitarian item offers ideal prerequisites for individual formation, often carried out in cooperation by stove builders and locksmiths or potters. Often the oven builder is also an artistic handcrafter himself. Recently several experienced firms have taken up oven building again. They offer their models in catalogs and also direct the assembly on the scene or build individual ovens under contract, using their own and others' designs. It is rewarding to visit such a firm and follow the production process—it resembles a visit to an artist's studio. Such an experience can create a very personal relationship to such a handcrafted object. The collaboration among artists on oven models has a long tradition, not only in creating unique items, but also in the design work for the models in pattern books, through which striking ovens were sent all over the world by mail order, up to the beginning of the twentieth century. The illustrated examples of ovens on the market, artistic objects made in small series, and simple or artistically unique pieces, can and should only indicate what formative possibilities the fireplace oven offers. In recent days, the available models have become much more extensive, both in terms of those that stress utility and those made as works of art. And the renaissance of the fireplace oven has just begun—a rebirth with a future.

An exception: This tile oven cannot only be used as an open fireplace—for its unusual form can also serve here as an effective inspiration.

Controlled fire: The traditional Danish oven (upper left) can also be opened. The design at left shows the fire and, in the safety lock, stresses the danger that can come from it.

Right: The tile oven as an energy block, which also allows a look at the open flames.
Architect: AGN, Bernhard Busch.

The classic "Franklin" stove has its optical volume supported a bit by the tiling in its surroundings.

This unit, with its three-dimensional effect, acts as a room divider between the dining and living areas.
Total design: Alois Juraschek.

Above: The finished fireplace as a decorative element with an effective heating function. Accent Kamine.

Rough steel plates: The architects have illustrated the motif of the total architecture of the house layout as an oven.
Architects: Independent Planning Group Neues Bauen from the U. K.

Left: A time-tested Danish fireplace oven, which can also be operated with an open fire. The body and smokestack are carefully detailed in relation to the wall panels, the bookshelf, and the floor material. Architect: Peter Berten.

Fireplace ovens often show something exaggeratedly rustic in their formation. This clear form is very different; its proportions and details bespeak a capable designing hand. Architect: Mechtild Friedrich-Schoenberger.

The fireplace ovens shown on the following pages come from one manufacturer, to whom not only perfect heating technology but also the esthetic experience matters. All fireplaces are heated with wood—without a fire rack or bottom air. The ash production in this form of combustion is extremely meager, amounting to only 1 to 2% of the quantity of burned wood. All fireplace ovens are made with double walls and consist of sheet steel up to 10 millimeters thick. A covering of firebrick 40 millimeters thick provides long-lasting and even heat supply through convection and radiation (about 80% effective). These stoves—though with a lower degree of effectiveness—can also be used as open fireplaces.

Below: Kubus Model
Right: Bocca Model. Matten.

The Visor heating fireplace awakens the most varied associations. Here the cabinet containing the flames, which guarantees safety, also reminds one to use it cautiously. Matten.

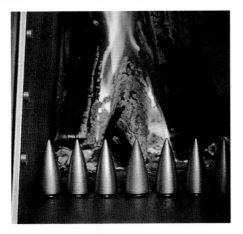

In this oven too, the fire motif provides warmth and warning of danger by its formation, its charm being a dialog between strict oven form and aggressive pointed rods. Matten.

Here a kayak was the model for the shape and surface formation. The oven relates to any room situation through its shaped bottom plate—as an unusual three-dimensional heat producer. Matten.

Left: The heating fireplace as a decorative steel structure, its form suiting the clean forms of this newly built environment. Matten.

FIREPLACE ACCESSORIES

To keep a fireplace fire burning well, setting up a harmonious firewood formation to attain a stimulating fire appearance, requires a specific treatment of the fire. It also gives pleasure to be able to manipulate the play of the flames to their best symbolic effect, all from a safe distance of course. For this to work, to maintain and enjoy in the forms of the fire, firewood must be piled up, and fire and ashes need to be carefully stirred and removed some time after the fire has been put out. Only a few simple practices are needed for this, and they can be performed with, but also without, the traditional fireplace utensils. For some, these utensils are always in the way, are unhandy, too big or too small; for others they are an essential component of fireplace ambience, never mind whether they are used or not. Actually used or even worn-out fireplace tools, though, are seen very rarely among the readily available utensils that are seen beside many fireplaces. Purists despise them; traditionalists long for them; many fireplace fans simply cannot find the formally and functionally satisfying equipment for their own fireplace, which they built with so much dedication. The offerings are also rather one-sided, for both the modern and the historic-oriented repertoire of forms. As a compromise, one can make do without the actual utensils—a small shovel and broom do the job too, and for straightening the logs, a piece of wood can be used as a poker, or two as usable tongs. On the other hand, a fire screen is very practical, as is a container in which the required quantity of wood is dried for the fire at room temperature—then it burns better. As for the individual equipment: *Grates* and *andirons* are not essential for starting a fire or good burning, but they supply the fire with air from below at the start of the burning process, and if they are set according to the space, they keep the firewood from falling out. If the heads of the andirons are formed properly, for example, decorated with gleaming brass parts, they can constitute a decorative element both when the fireplace is in use and when the hearth is unpleasantly empty. If they are the right size, they also create another heat-radiating surface. If there is no *wood holder* built into the actual fireplace wall—and this makes sense, as insects are always brought into the house along with the wood and make themselves at home in the warm air—then any suitable container, such as a wicker basket or a bucket of any kind of material can be used to hold the wood. If they suit the style of the fireplace, these wood holders can be a becoming decorative element with a justified function. A really sensible piece of equipment is the *spark curtain* of an open fireplace. Here too, there are a number of variations. As an element made of woven iron grid, brass or glass, they allow the flames to be seen or serve as an integrated fire screen in the form of a metal curtain that is installed at the top or side of the fire pit and can be pulled out when needed, providing effective protection against flying sparks or burning pieces of wood.

The spark curtain as a practical fire protector that projects forward. It can be made of glass as a visual "nothing" or be seen as a formative element that belongs to the fireplace, part of a centuries-old decorative tradition.

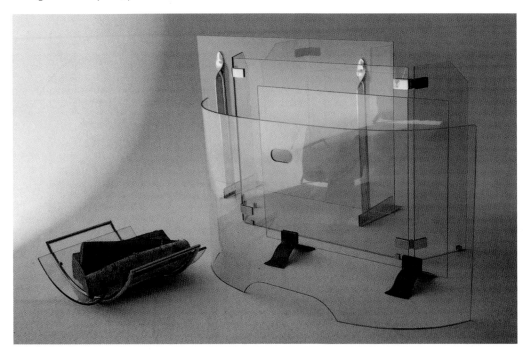

Baskets and bowls made of many materials are suitable for holding wood. The more closed the container, the less dust it catches. In any case, the capacity should be big enough to hold a sufficient quantity of wood to bring the fire up to room temperature. Andirons and grates make starting a fire easier, but are not necessary. The integrated ash box makes cleaning easier and simultaneously limits the air from below. The result is slower burning.

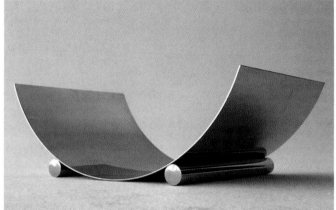

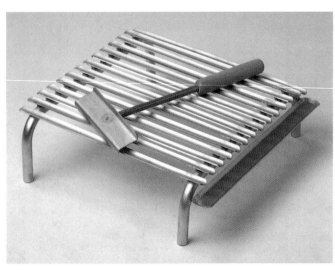

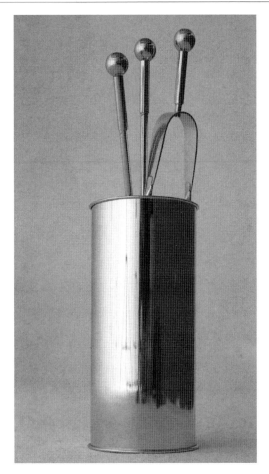

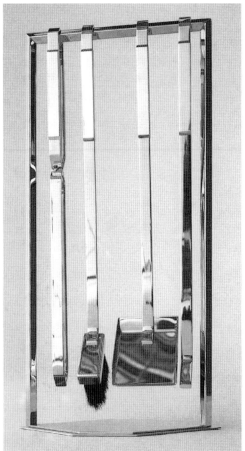

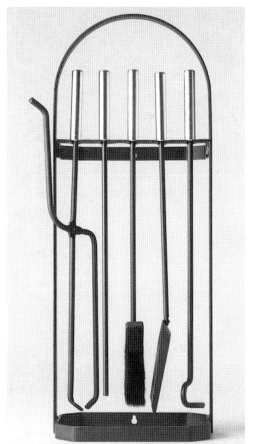

Fireplace tools are
very decorative, to be
sure, though their use
requires some skill and
enthusiasm—a normal hand
broom and a shovel will also
serve. Only the fire tongs
protect against touching the
hot firewood.

The spark curtain can also be a particularly decorative fireplace accessory; when appropriately formed it convincingly covers the empty black fire pit and thus assures that the fireplace always provides a pleasing overall appearance, and also draws attention to itself even when a fire is not burning. As for the actual *fireplace tools,* there are different concepts. The *bellows* will be found in many sets. This decorative piece can easily be eliminated, for it is only used if the wood is not dry enough, the draft is too weak, or the wood was stacked improperly—thus it is a utensil that needs to be used only if mistakes were made in handling the wood or the fireplace. And if it constantly hangs on the tool rack, then it indicates this failing even when the fireplace is not being used. The *tongs* are useful for handling hot firewood, but the fire can also be brought to the right form with a piece of wood. The same applies to the *poker,* which certainly looks powerful when it hangs on one of the four hooks for the tools, but which can also be done without. A *shovel* and *broom* in their usual long forms are, as a rule, so badly shaped that one cannot properly clean a fireplace with these two devices, since the shovel is usually much too small and the broom with its long handle is hard to maneuver, especially with light, fleeting ashes. Any normal household dustpan with a small hand brush will be better suited for this necessary cleaning operation. Often the suspicion arises that the fireplace tools standing next to the fire have more of an alibi function and should indicate that the fireplace is actually used now and then. In any case, present-day fireplace tools do not seem to have awakened the genuine interest of designers—the number of models on the market is small and only seldom convincing. Hopefully, this will change—after all, we are just at the beginning of a newly awakening love for fireplaces.

ASPECTS OF FIREPLACE PLANNING

TYPES AND CHARACTERISTICS

The theme of this book is the fireplace in its three main types, as:
--a traditional open fireplace,
--a heating fireplace with hot-air cassette installation, or as a hot-water fireplace,
--a fireplace oven or stove.

The center of gravity is the fireplace in its original form as an open fireplace—despite or even because of its particular characteristics, including the negative ones. Next to the campfire, the open fireplace is the most uneconomical heating system, has the lowest degree of heating effect, is technically long obsolete, is very work-intensive in terms of fuel-holding, preparation, readiness, and in the removal of its ashes; with careless or downright wrong handling it can even be dangerous and damaging to the environment—but only then. At least this last argument can be overcome; the others cannot. Yet the open fireplace remains the most convincing type of fireplace, because it is the most impressive. Therefore the two other types are portrayed only through considerably fewer examples and less explanation of their effectiveness. Anyone who wants to get involved with details of alternative kinds of heating is urged to consult the specialist literature, which is rightfully dedicated on this subject, particularly to questions of effectiveness: optimal heat production, its degree of effectiveness, the subject of reducing emissions, reducing the volume of construction, ease of operation,

optimal price/performance ratio in the production of extra heating, and other utilitarian aspects of working with fire. With the open fireplace, things are different. Its fans and advocates know all the unattainable qualities of this only almost controlled type of fire; not only do they know them, but they take them willingly in the bargain. These fans even long for the disparate characteristics of the open fireplace. In dealing with the fireplace, its users do not look hopefully into a technological future, but emotionally into the distant and more distant past—back to the origins of dealing with the fascinating flames. The visible historical path began in caves, with the fire pit in the ground and the hearth, the smoke of which departed only through the unsealed roof. Already more cultivated, because it was based on a formative purpose, was the fireplace in the corner of a thick castle wall, with a hole in the wall over it through which the smoke could escape from the heated room, maybe not completely but at least very well. This situation remained until, at last, the working principle of the fireplace draft became known and was expressed in the structural form of the chimney—and the room was finally rid of smoke.

Since the exhaust gases, because of their higher temperature, are specifically lighter than the colder surrounding air, they are pushed upward. The greater the temperature difference and the higher the chimney, the stronger are the flow and draft by which the friction occurring in the smoke channels is overcome. This awareness has meanwhile been reflected in the installation of smooth steel pipes or ceramic installations in the chimney.

The technical end points of this historical development reached at present are included in the "Guidelines in the Building of Open Fireplaces" published by the chimney sweeps' organization in 1979, according to which the building offices base their regulation of building permits.

The *open fireplace* can be erected either by a stove builder in the form of individual masonry, or merely installed as a readymade finished fireplace and connected to a chimney, and then brought into the desired form by coverings or frameworks. Readymade fireplaces are available for almost every room situation, one-, two- or even three-sided open types, made either of cast iron plates, fire bricks or concrete, with flues, smoke flaps and connecting stovepipes.

In principle, every open fireplace needs its own chimney draft, to which other fireplaces—including fireplaces above or below it in multi-story buildings—must not be attached. A short ascending smoke channel links the hearth with the chimney. The latter must be fitted to the hearth, the size of the fire opening, and the connecting pipe. All the components of the open fireplace may be made only of non-inflammable material and must retain their form. The bottom of the hearth is to be insulated against heat transfer to the cover, as also the side and back walls. Open fireplaces should always be operated under supervision and fired only with low-resin wood (see the "Fuel" chapter). Sufficient air supply for the fire must be guaranteed, for the oxygen supply is vital in making the fire burn well. It is best directly from outdoors, so that not too much already warmed inside air escapes through the chimney—with an average room size, there should be an air volume of some 500 cubic meters per hour, which also lets adjoining rooms cool off quickly. Air channels coming directly from outside are a relatively new technical addition to the traditional fireplace configuration, which is now being accepted even by decidedly traditional fireplace builders—not only for reasons of energy, but because not enough oxygen-rich fresh air would reach the fire because of the thickness of today's present window structure. Weariness and not feeling well would result, if not something worse.

Despite these little technical refinements of air supply, the heating effectiveness degree of an open fireplace is still something more than 10%--but heating is no longer its real purpose any more today. Satisfactory heating performance cannot be expected from the antiquated open fireplace. When the heating capacity is found to be insufficient, it can be helped by rebuilding the open fireplace into a *heating fireplace* by means of an added hot-air cassette, a fireplace ready to be installed, which is set into the existing fireplace opening in a small building operation, which does not generate much dirt. This process, moreover, is also well suited for reviving a non-functioning open fireplace. In a heating fireplace, the controlled fire burns behind closed glass doors, to be sure, but highly efficiently.

From the weakly performing radiation fireplace, the installation of a fireplace cassette creates a combination consisting of a radiation and convection aggregate that makes better fuel utilization possible and lets very little warm air escape into the chimney. Such heating installations result in a remarkably high degree of efficiency and are thus an efficient alternative to an open fireplace, even in transition times as well as when the heating system breaks down or insufficient energy is produced in an emergency, especially since they can also be used with their doors open as fireplaces.

The rebuilding process is very simple: Hot-air cassettes, available in varying dimensions for all customary fireplace sizes, are inserted into the existing fire area and sealed to the brickwork so that no room air can flow out to the chimney. The heating principle, thus changed, is simple and effective: The double-walled cassette is made of sheet steel or cast iron. In the hollow between the walls, the cool air flowing in at the bottom of the cassette is warmed by the heated metal and streams back out at the top of the cassette as a heating medium, while the exhaust gases are conducted directly into the chimney. The hot-air cassettes work completely by the air-circulation principle. Ventilators can also be installed to intensify the hot-air circulation. The closable glass doors turn the once-open fireplace into a steadily burning oven in which, depending on the buyer's wishes and the equipment of the device, not only wood but also turf and briquettes can be burned. In this way the heating fireplace with a hot-air cassette attains an effect of some 70% at a production of some 15 kW, which also suffices to heat larger rooms. The rebuilding of an open fireplace into a heating fireplace is to be discussed by the district chimney sweep before the work begins, and requires his approval. The installation itself must be done by a specialist firm. In no case can the existing fireplace structure be manipulated, such as by adapting the sidewalls to create the space needed for the cassette. Any change to the fireplace structure, its stability, or its insulation for bordering structures, holds the danger of later overheating, and possibly even fire.

In the planning of a new heating fireplace—the very concept indicates that in this construction the heating, not the contemplative enjoyment of an open fire, is most important—the technical equipment can be refined further, improving performance and effect.

There are two different types of apparatus, these being the *hot air* or *hot water* heating for the fireplace. The operating principle of the *hot-air fireplace* corresponds to that of the heating cassette, but in a new construction it can be fitted to the dimensions, equipment, and heating needs of the room and sometimes of the whole house. These heating fireplaces are also hot-air ovens, in which the play of the flames takes place with regulated burning behind glass doors. The operation utilizes circulating air from the room or fresh air from outdoors. The circulating process has the disadvantage that the air for combustion is taken out of the room—to be sure, only in small quantities and not comparably with an open fireplace, but the room air is circulated more per hour and thus becomes very dry. Finally, an unpleasant smell can even spread, because dust particles from the moving air constantly float onto the hot oven walls.

Thus the closed circulating air or fresh air principle is more advantageous. Here air from outside is ducted to the heating fireplace through a channel, is warmed on the hot walls, and then streams into the room as warm air. At the same time, the used room air is sucked into the fireplace as combustion air and led out via the chimney. The breathing air is richer in oxygen and not so dry, and the dust development in the room is largely eliminated. These heating fireplaces can also be upgraded by installing air blowers. Since they can also be used with open doors as old-fashioned open fireplaces, every fireplace needs its own chimney draft.

A particularly high-performance variant of the heating fireplace is the *hot-water fireplace,* which includes a heating apparatus with a large-surface network of pipes, which can be connected to the hot-water pipes of the central heating. Via a heat exchanger, the hot gases from the fire give their heat to the hot water, which in turn is conducted, when its temperature is hot enough, to the circulating system of the heating and automatically turns it off—the fireplace oven takes over the heating operation as radiation heating with a physiologically pleasant effect. The degree of effectiveness of this hot-water heating fireplace is about 80%, thanks to the good energy utilization of the fuel through the heating medium of water and simultaneous use of hot-air convection. The installation of such a heating fireplace must also be approved by the district's master chimney sweep. Because of the heavy weight of this fireplace (up to 300 kg), the construction and static circumstances of the location need to be checked, and the covers may need to be strengthened. A specialist firm should, in any case, do the technical installation; only the concluding decorative exterior, which is touched by neither exhaust gases nor high temperatures, can be done personally. Since this technical refinement is not inexpensive, the investment is only rewarding if the heating fireplace is often in operation and clearly decreases the fuel consumption of the central heating system. Whether such a heating system is permitted with wood or other fuels should be discussed in advance with the district chimney sweep.

Unfortunately, in such heating fireplaces, intended so much for their function, one still finds only a few convincing, modern and similarly varied forms as those of the open fireplace or closed standing oven, for which there is a long creative tradition. This may be another explanation for why many builders still prefer an individually designed fireplace with all its functional shortcomings, instead of turning to what is offered in the trade, where a certain refinement of form is lacking. But this can change quickly if renowned builders, designers, architects, and interior decorators would finally take up this building task, small, to be sure, but rewarding, as has already taken place in fireplace oven building.

Fireplace ovens are sources of heat that, as decorative individual pieces, operate similarly to fireplace cassettes, work overwhelmingly by the convection principle, and attain a degree of effectiveness of over 70%. They exist in two different forms. One has self-closing doors that do not allow operation with open doors, but do allow that a chimney draft can be used by more than one fireplace. The other type operates with a fire chamber either open or closed, and always requires its own chimney draft. The hearth of such a fireplace oven is usually equipped with a grate and ash box, so that briquettes can be burned as well as wood. Since the capacity of fireplace ovens is usually limited and the constant use amounts to three to four kilograms of wood, such an oven must be fueled several times a day. On the basis of this usually meager volume of fire space and surface heating, the small ceramic or iron fireplace ovens are not suited for use as constantly burning ovens. Rather they should be used in the spring and fall, but not completely replace the central heating.

Their performance of up to 19 kW, though, is considerable, and suffices to heat a room volume of 300 cubic meters. The installation of a fireplace oven also requires the approval and acceptance of the district chimney sweep.

Each of the described fireplace types has, along with its specific emotional charm, also very definite, clearly defined advantages and disadvantages, which do not make the decision to choose one system or another all that difficult.

THE LOCATION OF THE FIREPLACE

There are no firm rules as to the "right" location of a fireplace, but several basic aspects can make the decision for the suitable location easier. With an established building situation, it is simple to locate the fireplace on a free side of the already existing chimney. The official master chimney sweep can provide information as to whether such a possibility exists and also allows fresh-air intake for the fireplace from outdoors.

If the position of the chimney does not suit the desired positioning, then a new chimney, suited for the architecture of the house, can be built on the outer wall. The situation is simpler for a house that is to be built new, for the planning can include consideration for the fireplace, and perhaps even make the needed chimney an especially decorative element of the total architecture, as was an architectural tradition into the 1930s.

Along with the construction situation, the functional aspects of the fireplace remain to be explained. Should it be primarily a decorative element in the interior décor, or should its function as a heating fireplace take precedence? Then the location will surely depend on practical standpoints, such as convenient and largely dirt-free wood or fuel supplying and ash removal. Since the daily consumption of wood can easily exceed twenty kilograms, surely this argument should not be overlooked.

Above all, though, the location of a planned heating fireplace certainly should be determined according to which room it is most needed in and thus gives the best service.

For the fans of open fireplaces, these aspects will have no significance, or at least a minor one; for them the formative aspect will be decisive for the design and building of the fireplace—for the necessary chimney solution, large-scale rebuilding measures may even be accepted. If the esthetic effect is paramount, it should be considered whether the fireplace should be the visual center of one's own fireplace room or a decorative element in the living room, dining room or hall, so as to give entering guests a feeling of inviting warmth and pleasant coziness. Perhaps if rebuilding is necessary anyway, two or three fireplaces should be installed at the start, for a bedroom can also be an ideal location for a fireplace.

Along with the search for the best-suited place for a burning fireplace, one should also ask oneself what effect it will have on the room when the fireplace is not in operation, and how the fireplace will affect a possible later change in the room's function. Experience has shown that many fireplace fans have a firm formal concept of "their" fireplace. Will this fireplace then create the intended ambience, the right point of view? And do the fireplace design, room size, proportions, furnishings, and décor unite in a total layout that enhances the atmosphere? In the end, a fireplace is not a movable piece of furniture that can simply be stuck in the attic if one does not like it.

Since the fireplace represents a very important, often even dominant architectural element in the house, and above and beyond that amounts to a substantial investment, which can add up to several or many thousands of dollars depending on its architectural quality, it should be considered whether an architect or interior decorator should be consulted about its location and formation.

If constructive changes to the building become necessary because of rebuilding measures for a new chimney, or for the installation of a heavy oven, or if the façade is changed by building regulations, an architect is required in any case to make the plans, set up the appropriate building contract, and obtain authorization from the master chimney sweep.

All aspects of the practicability of a fireplace have their justification. And yet the question of good feeling and comfort, the decorative effect and particular ambience of a fireplace room will always be paramount, for if these characteristics are lacking and the fireplace has no actual aura, one day it will be scarcely or never used. But this is not what is meant by the formulation of DIN 18895, "the fireplace should be a fire site for occasional use", which regulates fireplace operation.

Viewpoint of the Fireplace Wall

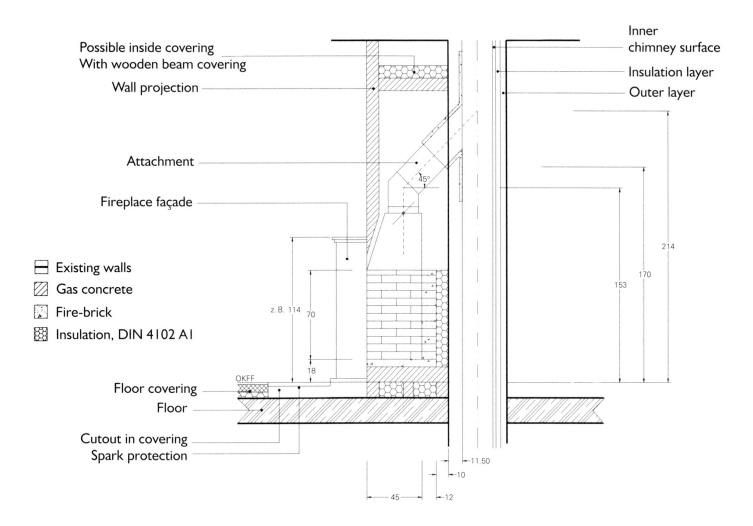

Possible inside covering
With wooden beam covering

Wall projection

Inner
chimney surface

Insulation layer

Outer layer

Attachment

45°

Fireplace façade

⊟ Existing walls

▨ Gas concrete

▦ Fire-brick

▤ Insulation, DIN 4102 A1

214

170

153

z. B. 114 70

18

OKFF

Floor covering

Floor

Cutout in covering
Spark protection

11.50

10

45   12

Functional cutaway drawing of a fireplace with hot air operation

1. Hot air ducting
2. Ventilator
3. Outside air
4. Room air
5. Hot air
6. Room air grid, can be regulated
7. Hot-air exit grid
8. Lowerable glass panel
9. Smokestack connection
10. Smoke flap
11. Isolation

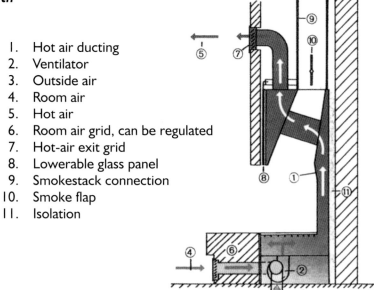

Vertical function cutaway of an open fireplace layout

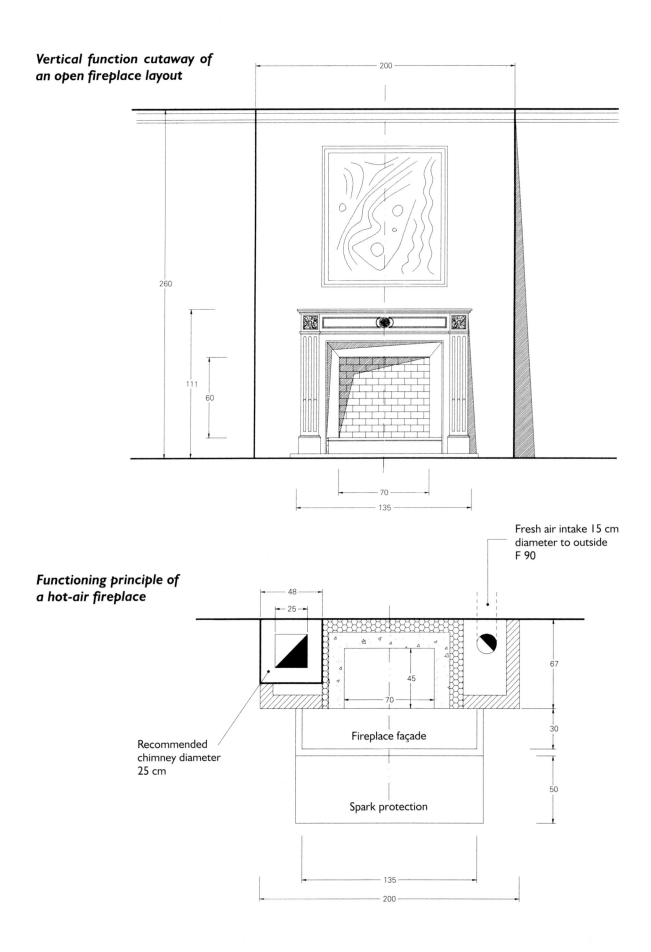

200

260

111

60

70

135

Fresh air intake 15 cm diameter to outside F 90

Functioning principle of a hot-air fireplace

48

25

45

70

67

30

50

Fireplace façade

Spark protection

Recommended chimney diameter 25 cm

135

200

HEARTH AND OPENING

The hearth, the opening that faces the room, the flue, and chimney form a functioning unit, the individual elements of which must be tuned very precisely to each other so that the fire in the fireplace can be ignited quickly and without trouble and can show an evenly glowing flame scene when lit. Beyond that, it should give off the desired quantity of radiating energy to the room—the larger the hearth opening, the greater the radiation—and not let combustion gases into the room in either the earlier or later phases. With open, readymade fireplaces, heating fireplaces, and heating ovens, there is much experience on hand. Dimensions and structures of the individual fireplace elements, the necessary chimney height and diameter are tested by the manufacturer, and such a fireplace burns well as a rule. The situation is different with individual fireplace designs that are erected only at the building site, and the functioning and effect of which must prove themselves. With such a design, a unique one, the architectural effect is paramount at first. Here the location of the installed hearth directly on the floor or raised, the size of the opening and the depth, as well as the surroundings, are the vital design criteria. The dominant formative means are the fireplace size, plasticity, and hearth opening, plus the material effect and color, which make up the complete effect of the fireplace as an answer to the room proportions. The technical-functional detail planning, in connection with the designing work, is thus the indispensable work of the fireplace builder, who also takes over the calculation and construction of the individual components. In addition, he provides the necessary data for the air intake channel, usually made up at the building site, the chimney, and, if necessary, the foundation. It is advisable to agree on the design concept early, including the planned materials for the fire pit and frame, so as to be able to form a picture of the necessary space for the fireplace mantel, including the insulating materials, the depth of the structure, and the size of the flue and the chimney. It goes without saying that the inner walls of the fire pit must be made of materials that will not burn: fire brick, tile, etc., that are also suitable for the chimney, or sheet steel—the idea is that these surfaces, along with their heat-radiating function, can also have an interesting esthetic effect if not utilized often. Thus one should recall the charm of old and also contemporary oven plates and the use of different stone formations, structures, or the installation of colorful glazed tiles. If the agreement between the designer and the fireplace builder has gone smoothly to the end of the planning, the fireplace will also draw well later. There are constructions that, despite all technical refinements and calculations, still need the almost mystic ability of the master builder, so that the piece of work, above and beyond its normal functioning, later reveals and "radiates" that certain something—the fireplace builder's handicraft still belongs to it.

FLUE

The flue is the necessary link between the hearth and the chimney. It lies hidden behind the vertical fireplace wall or is symbolically featured as an angled form narrowing to a funnel shape at the top. The hot gases arising in the hearth, with a temperature of up to 1000 degrees Celsius over the fire, mix with incoming air in the flue, and form the cloud of smoke that enters the flue as a gaseous mix. Here is it hastened by the increasing reduction in area and, cooled to a temperature of 100 degrees, conducted into the chimney. To make a complete acceptance of the smoke gases possible, the flue opening over the fire should be somewhat larger than the surface occupied by the fire, because the cloud of smoke expands upward. But if the flue opening is too small or the draft too weak, the smoke gases push out of the fire pit into the room, which not only make the air smell worse but also blackens the fireplace wall and spreads the soot over the entire room.

With the right balance among the hearth size, the flue, and chimney, the flue can always take in at least the volume of gas that can be conducted away by the chimney. Along with the size of the flue, the temperature of the smoke gases when they enter the flue determines the strength of the draft. Thus the distance between the top of the fire and the bottom of the flue must be chosen so that the temperature of the gases in the flue is high enough to create the needed updraft, the draft in the chimney. If the temperature is too low, the smoke pushes back into the room.

The quality of the combustion process in the fireplace depends decisively on the proportions of the flue, the hearth size, and the opening to the room. If the flue hangs too deep, the fireplace draws very well but the play of flames is not so beautiful to see, and less radiant warmth comes out of the fireplace into the room.

In the heating fireplace, though, which creates both radiant heat and convection heat, the radiating surface of the hearth is not so decisive for the heating effect. The typical shape of the hearth is thus a relatively small horizontal rectangle.

Besides the hearth and the flue, the chimney length above the fire, the shape and size of its cross-section are decisive for the draft of the fireplace. If a fireplace is built later, then there is the difficulty of finding a free draft in the chimney. In old buildings the chimney drafts have often been filled or walled up. They must then be either opened—a laborious and expensive undertaking—or replaced by a new chimney—usually a simple heat-insulated steel pipe.

Unfortunately, these readymade chimneys often disturb the appearance of the façade, and it would be rewarding to recall the especially decorative chimney types of, for example, the twenties, or the chimney types of British and American single-family houses, in which the necessary function became a convincing formative element, which often gave the house a particular character: The fireplace chimney as a symbol of coziness.

The fireplace builder is responsible for the right function, the architect for the shape—a collaboration that can be demanding, for it is not always easy, what with the existing data on an old chimney, to fulfill the wishes for the size and shape of the connected fireplace.

FRESH AIR INTAKE

In light of several factors, the comfort in the room containing the fireplace, the heating effect, and the even burning of the fire, the right arrangement and dimensions of the fresh air intake takes on a vital importance. In any case, the fire needs some 360 cubic meters of air per hour for normal operation, and quantity that, with today's tightly closable windows and doors, can no longer be supplied by the natural air exchange between inside and outside or from adjoining rooms. It would also not be very practical in terms of energy to suck cold outside air through the nearest window or the whole house to provide enough combustion air. The radiant warmth of the fireplace would not come near sufficing to make up the resulting loss of energy. As a result, the air warmed by the heating system would be sucked out to feed the fire in the open fireplace and then take the shortest way out via the chimney. To prevent this, the air needed for both the open and closed operation of the fireplace is brought in by its own air supply channel. The dimensions of this channel are calculated by the fireplace builder on the basis of the hearth size and the chimney draft. The air channel should be heat-insulated and be able to suck the air directly from outside by the shortest possible route.

From the sketch to the design:
Planning a combined hot-air fireplace
and tile oven (see photo, page 49).
Architect: Gert M. Mayr-Kleber,
Vienna

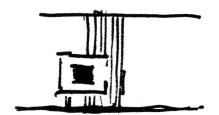

Before igniting the fire, one opens the air exit flap in the flue and the air intake flap for fresh air, and closes them both as soon as possible after putting out the fire, so as to avoid unnecessary heat transfer out of the building. For this reason, the air intake channel should not, as was long customary, duct the combustion air from the cellar, as cold outdoor air would then stream in, which would lead to heightened and easily avoided energy use.

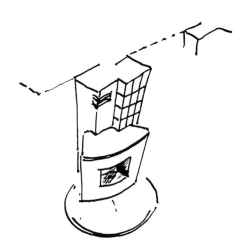

Although the heating fireplace with a fire burning behind closed glass doors need only about one-tenth the combustion air of an open fireplace, it is still advisable to install its own air intake for this type of fireplace, especially since this type is chosen for the purpose of saving energy and not for the pure joy of an open fire. Since the air intake openings in the fireplace itself—in the sides, back wall or base plate of the hearth—require a size that cannot be ignored, planning where these air intakes will be least disturbing must be done according to the type of fireplace, hearth size, and layout. If fresh air is ducted directly into the hearth, the entire radiant warmth of the heating of the room in which the fireplace is located benefits. The hearth size, chimney, air intake, and diameter thus become a finely tuned system, so that the fireplace works in the desired way. This is of particular significance for an individual design in which no averaged and tested system can be used.

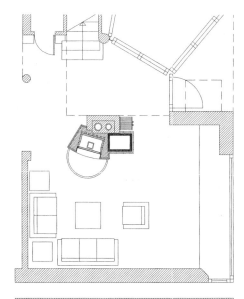

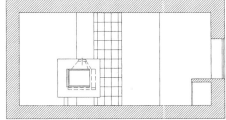

DESIGN

FORM, PROPORTIONS, STYLE, AND MATERIALS

When buying a fireplace oven or a readymade fireplace, the decision process for its shape and size proceeds similarly to that used when buying a piece of furniture. One can look at the company's stock, evaluate it, take the measurements, and estimate the later room effect by the dimensions. Whoever still cannot decide on the basis of such concepts might under the circumstances, if it is not too difficult, even have one set up for testing. This process is very customary, as when buying furniture, with the costs of work and transportation to be paid if one does not buy it. When planning an individual fireplace, the situation is different. Here there is no full-size model; the fireplace conception must grow slowly in size and shape and take on contours. As with every design, there are certain time-tested work processes that one should use in planning a fireplace and, in fact, not only consider oneself but also discuss with architects, interior decorators or fireplace builders. The more aspects of the planning are made clear in the preliminary stage, the shorter the designer's work and the lower the cost will be. With a relatively small design task, such as a fireplace requires, the planner will usually want to charge according to his time—and this will amount to some 150 Euros per hour.

At the start of the design consideration, the question of what function the fireplace shall fulfill will arise—regardless of whether it is planned for the living room, dining room, kitchen, den, bedroom or bath. Is it to have mainly decorative

purposes or take on a real heating function, and above all, how often will it presumably be used? This question can be of importance in terms of maintaining the fire and storing the wood purposefully. Its location is a decisive aspect. Should a fireplace be the dominant visual aspect of the room, or rather an additional decorative element, such as in an entry hall, where it has only an inviting and stimulating function and only makes a momentary impression on the viewer? Or should it, as the visual center of the room, be placed in the center of the room or planned so that the fireplace can function as a room divider, perhaps separating the eating area from the actual living room? Naturally, the location of the chimney plays a role in locating the fireplace, but even if it is not exactly in the desired place, makeshift designs that work can often be created, such as moving the stovepipe or hanging the ceiling and building in a ventilator, in order, for example, to be able to use the fireplace as an open type in the room. If it is set up in front of a wall, the latter needs to be doubled and the smoke channel to the chimney hidden behind it, if the fireplace's body will not project far into the room. On the one hand, the size of the fireplace and the hearth opening will be determined technically because the chimney size, height, and draft allow only certain hearth dimensions, and on the other hand, they are determined above all by their function: A heating fireplace, as a rule, has a relatively small hearth opening, which is closed by glass doors—the visual size of such a fireplace can be increased only by the total volume of the fireplace structure. This is also true of open fireplaces, whose hearth openings cannot be very big, on account of the existing chimney's dimensions.

A further functional viewpoint concerns the air supply through a channel and the draft-free situation in the room. If draft air can disturb the smoke outflow, or the fireplace will be located right next to a door, it is susceptible to disturbance and will subsequently be used rarely, and soon exhaust itself as a "cold fire". When the functional aspects of the fireplace location and the related effect are made clear, the designing begins, and the step-by-step development of the form along with it. It can help to build a model of the fireplace room in 1:10 scale or use a computer simulation in which the room effects, proportions, and even the optical appearance of the materials can be included.

Standing or hanging free in the room, the fireplace will always have a dominant effect, similar to a three-dimensional object: the fireplace becomes a work of art. Its formation should be appropriately impressive, not only as applies to the actual body of the fireplace, but also in relation to the volume of the room around it. On the other hand, if it is planned for one wall, it must be decided whether the fireplace is to stand against the wall like a piece of furniture, with a three-dimensional form with a straight or curved smokestack, whether the entire fireplace is to be set into the wall or, mostly hidden, be arranged behind a fireplace front coming slightly out from the wall. This amounts to the classic form in a wainscoted fireplace room. Even if the framed open fire determines the actual function in this case, its effect still recedes before the total ensemble of such interior décor.

This brings up the question of whether the fireplace should, with its form, determine the impression made by the room or rather be a restrained decorative element, almost hidden, but still able to be filled with a living fire when so desired. An important effect of the fireplace is made by the arrangement of the fire opening. Set directly at floor level, it summons up antique associations: the fireplace as a necessary fire site in the original sense, and with dimensions that also conjure up roasting meat and a heavy iron pot hanging from the flue. If the hearth opening, on the other hand, is raised above floor level and set about at sitting level, this stresses the dwelling aspect of the fire, at which the gaze can focus while seated—and it also makes operating easier, for one does not have to bend so low when putting in the firewood. After the calculation of the most favorable location for the fireplace and the decision of the height of the hearth opening, there come the shaping, the determination of its size, and the surface formation, as well as the choice of materials. Here the existing room size, proportions, and furnishings can be connecting points for the shaping, but so is the desire to let the fireplace itself serve as the dominant element in the room, to which all the other aspects of the interior décor should be subordinated.

At this stage of the planning, to be sure, the spectrum of design possibilities is broad: It extends from individual designs via references to classic modern forms and fantastic, unusual designs, to the rustic elements, the replicas of old, classic fireplace frames and real antiquities, costly mantelpieces from various lands and epochs in fashion. As numerous as the possibilities of present-day formation are, the forms of historic fireplace frames are just as rich in variety, whether they are genuine antiques or artistic reproductions. Also among the various forms and styles are the interior-decorative effects of the various materials for the fireplace itself, the hearth opening and the fireplace body. The spectrum ranges from the clean, simple white projection from the wall via the neat body that is formed in color, to a material choice in which the structure, color or particular character of the components or building materials should dominate. Traditionally, the masonry of the wall, in the most varied sizes, is a classic material for the hearth and fireplace body.

Along with the richly varied formats, the various colors and surface structures offer charming design possibilities, as do different glazes, the patina of old bricks, and the numerous connecting links that can be formed and shaped with the bricks.

Another material with a long tradition in tile ovens, but which has been neglected in open fireplaces since the 1920s, is the ceramic tile, or even the historic tile, available in countless patterns, formats, colors, and surfaces—an ideal formative element for the fireplace wall or frame, and also available as an old and antique material with charming craquelure or in painted form.

The formative possibilities of natural stone are numerous, from the strict and simple to the very luxurious, with both modern and classic styles based on the masonry tradition from the age of Baroque and pseudo-classicism. In the use of natural stone, many present-day designs are limited to the combination of readily available plates. But besides its variety of colors, natural stone also offers the possibility of profiling, which allows not only the sculptor's artistry but also machine shaping into the most varied forms, and at remarkably affordable prices. The visual charm of natural stone can also be developed by various working techniques such as polishing or piercing the surfaces or leaving them rough.

In the naturalness of its look, wood comes close to natural stone as a material. Here associations with historic wall paneling with integrated fireplaces are awakened, carved fireplace frames of softwood, such as the British brought to their highest point, and that can still be had today as antiques in many versions, chiefly from the period around 1800, plus replicas of these forms.

They not only produce a reflection of history, but are still attractive today as independent, handcrafted frames because of their artistic refinements, becoming all the lovelier with years of use and gradual patina development. Along with its historical echoes, wood can also be made into the most varied forms for contemporary styling, for whole fireplace walls as well as just a molding, on which small works of art or personal mementos can find a decorative place. Similarly to natural stone, wood has formative possibilities in terms of the most varied types of wood, their graining, coloring, and texture that extend far beyond the use of simple veneers and readymade plate material. But wood, like natural stone, is a material that unveils its whole charm only when it is applied by a capable hand, in the design as well as the handcrafting. This applies in a similar way to the relatively new material of concrete.

Concrete, like clay, is an ideal building material for individual three-dimensional shaping. In its natural surface structure and in colored forms it has the same effect as artistically worked plastic. The field of concrete formation has been given too little attention to date.

At first glance, metal is similarly brittle to concrete in its working value. Like wood or stone, it offers a great variety of material with great charm. Fine metals like copper and brass can be worked relatively easily and with great variety. One can shape them, use them on the surface, stamp, brush, polish or use them in a combination of different crafting possibilities to give the fireplace a frame that directs the eye to the flames; its polished surfaces pick up and reflect the flickering of the flames. At the same time, such picture-frame surroundings form a decorative viewpoint even when no fire is burning in the fireplace. Brass and copper, though, cannot be shaped and brought to an effect only in the traditional handcrafting techniques, but are also used for contemporary forms. Likewise iron, steel, and bronze, which in addition to their functioning as historical examples, contain material characteristics that can be brought out today in extremely decorative forms.

Thus one should always consider that all of these materials, such as bricks, ceramics, natural stone, metals and alloys, wood, and even concrete offer certain qualities to the employed artisan, artist or architect.

THE AUTHORIZATION PROCESS

In the framework of simplification for smaller building projects, such as the erection of a fireplace, most of the German states have ceased to require a building permit as well as the authorization process for the building of fireplaces up to a listed heating performance of 50 kW, as long as no further structural changes are made to the building. Changing the façade by building a new chimney or constructive changes inside the building for static reasons, on the other hand, require authorization. Most of the fireplaces and fireplace ovens available in the trade have a capacity of only 5 to 15 kW and thus do not require a permit in those states. But this does not mean that the building and use of fireplaces were completely freed from all authorization. Rather the decision level was vested in the private industrial institution of the district master chimney sweep. He is to be consulted before the work begins, to find out whether a fireplace connection with the existing chimney system is possible and allowable, which sizes can be combined with an existing chimney cross-section, or whether cross-section changes are necessary or a new chimney can be built. If no individual draft exists, and if none is to be built, the possibility of connecting a fireplace oven of Type 1 to an existing draft remains. This type of fireplace can be operated only in a closed condition, as self-closing fire-pit doors prevent wrong usage, so that neither combustion gases nor glowing embers can come out in other fireplaces and lead to problems or even damage. If only one draft exists, this variant of the closed fireplace oven is still an alternative. Besides the basic approval, the builder is also required to have the orderly construction and safe functioning of the fireplace checked by the appropriate district master chimney sweep and finally have the building measures certified. Only then may the fireplace be put into action.

COSTS OF THE FIREPLACE

One must reckon with the following prices (gross end prices) for the building of a fireplace: The simple fireplace-oven requires an investment of 3000 Euros plus some 500 Euros for the chimney connection and mounting; large and decorative examples cost progressively more. Tile-oven fireplaces, for example, can scarcely be had for less than 10,000 Euros. For a simple, open, ready-made fireplace, assembled on site, 3000 Euros should be expected; the version with hot-air equipment costs at least 4500 Euros. The open fireplace that is built on site to an individual design must be acquired for some 4500 Euros in a simple version with cleaned walls, and the version with heating equipment will cost about 6000 Euros. To these sums must sometimes be added the renovation work in the area of the location and the costs of the electricians, together some 1000 to 1500 Euros. For more elaborate individual designs, one can add to the basic prices of the firing unit the price of the fireplace frame, ranging from 1500 Euros for a rough plaster mantel to 3000 to 5000 for a wooden frame and some 6000 to 10,000 Euros for a natural stone frame.

If the mounting of these frames, which are usually decorated with cast iron or brass fittings, is especially work-intensive, one must reckon on another 2000 Euros. Historical fireplace frames, bought from special antique dealers or firms that handle old building and decorating materials, are found for 10,000 Euros and up, depending on their age, size, and quality, and rare, especially splendid specimens can go over 50,000 Euros, while in rare cases, such as designs by renowned architects of the eighteenth and nineteenth centuries, or very old, superb sculptures can even reach 100,000 Euros. Rare, high-quality works of art have their price, especially if they have good provenance. But a valuable antique not only maintains its value but, in a disassembled state, can be resold, sometimes amounting to a significant investment.

If a fireplace is designed by an architect or created by an artist—there are also outstandingly lovely examples of this, all the way to the newest building history—the fee for the design must be added. The costs to be expected for these individual fireplaces, at whatever height, should be estimated in the total budget before building begins and fixed in a building contract, so that there are no disagreements later as to the cost of the work. This is also true of the work of an architect who supervises the building site from the designing to the final acceptance. For totals under 50,000 Euros he can work out the fee with the buyer; if the building costs are higher, then the fee will be calculated according to the tax laws for architects. To what extent the architect's fees alone should add up, and what form of payment is chosen, should be agreed on in writing by the involved parties in an architect's contract before the work begins.

CONSTRUCTION

PREPARATION AND PROCEDURE

The extent of the building work, its duration in time, and the preparation of the building site for the subsequent building of the fireplace should already be considered in the planning stage. The master chimney sweep, as the first to give advice and authorization, has the opportunity during the fireplace installation to check the extent of the building measures for the chimney connection. The actual planning of the fireplace builder, or with an individual design, is what the architect has to base work on. Appearance and detail drawings to 1:10 or 1:20 scale give information on the dimensions of the situation on the building site, and thus also on what preparatory work is necessary before the actual building of the fireplace can begin. For a simple fireplace oven, which requires only a chimney connection, it must just be determined whether the building site is suitable, the chimney connection possible, and the oven can be set up without danger of the radiating heat warming adjoining components and furnishings too much. Then only a hole through the wall to the chimney needs to be made, the exhaust duct installed, insulated and closed with a cuff. After five to six hours of building time the fireplace oven is ready for use.

The situation is different for an open fireplace that is built up by hand. Here a preliminary static test of the existing floor is necessary, as the weight of such a fireplace can easily amount to five hundred kilograms and cause unacceptable bending of the flooring. Next it should be tested whether electric lines run through the fireplace area and must be moved by the electrician, of whether new outlets have to be installed in the fireplace wall area. One must decide whether the fresh-air ducting should be installed below, for example, in the cellar, or through the wall to the outside, where the air intake opening in the façade is to be marked. In this case one should look for a place where such a blemish in the façade will not be noticed much.

After taking care of these technical preparations, one should ascertain the extent of the materials and their presumed weight, and discussion with the architect or the construction firm as to whether the materials can be delivered through the house or if it is recommended that they be delivered from outdoors. The water supply to the building site should also be considered; if possible, this supply should come from outside via a garden hose, to avoid unnecessary trips through the house by the workers. The high weight of the material makes it necessary to divide the individual components over the building area on wooden floors in old or single-family houses, so as to avoid overloading spots and thus avoid causing the floor to bend. Possible damage will not show during the storage time, but only later when the floor is unburdened.

Then within a few hours cracks in the floorboards will form; they can be removed only with a lot of trouble—and then in the ceiling below, in which absolutely no building dust must fall. When the arrangement of the building site is planned for preparation, material delivery, and storage, thought should be given to dust settling during the building time, and appropriate measures should be taken, likewise for waste removal, which can be done, for example, via a covered chute to the outside.

While installing a simple fireplace oven usually takes only one day, the building and assembly time of a masonry fireplace, including drying, and the necessary electronics and the decorative work of the painter can take up to three weeks. When artisans from several companies go in and out for three weeks, do demolition work, build stone walls, some of which have to be broken or cut to size, mix cement, water stones, saw boards, do cleaning and piecework, and then painting and decoration, then on such a "real" building site only practical and proper work should be done, providing the same room is not still being occupied. Thus it is recommended that the building site be separated from the occupied area with dust walls, so that the building dust that has to fall will be largely limited to one area. And since materials must be delivered again and again during the building time—in particular, in rebuilding for a subsequent fireplace installation, the unexpected has to be expected—then the access to the building site should be from outside if possible, such as by a mobile scaffolding. In the end, this is less expensive than having to renovate the entire stairwell and the adjoining rooms after the building is done.

When the fireplace is finished after a few weeks and can be put into service, and the encroachment of the construction work can quickly be forgotten, it would make sense to have thought out the building process to the end in advance, so as to estimate the extent of the work and time involved. Most builders thus find out that is saves labor for them to entrust the planning and development of the fireplace installation, from a certain size on, to an architect. He takes over the necessary integrative function for the various firms involved, which generally think and work only in terms of their own professional limits. With a fireplace, though, that should also fulfill the formal wishes of the builder, the careful finishing of every detail is especially vital—after all, the viewer's gaze is concentrated on the fireplace wall when a fire is burning on the hearth. Then uneven spots in the details can be very annoying.

It will be shown below how extensive the fireplace-building measures can be: Before the work starts in the house, a small device may be set up with an elevator to transport materials. A dust barrier may be set up in the fireplace room, or the doors of a completely vacant room may be taped to prevent the building dust from invading the whole house. To prepare the actual building site, floor coverings, wall installations and all flammable materials, plus electric fixtures, must be removed or repositioned. After that the work of building up the fire pit begins, along with the attached air intake ducts and perhaps circulators, or the installation of the heating unit. Then comes the installation of the flue, with a careful opening of the chimney, followed by the precise connection with it. Floors, walls, and ceilings in the neighborhood of the fireplace must be protected against heat radiation with the necessary insulation, and the floor must then be made ready to beat the entire weight of the fireplace. In apartment houses, sound-dampening materials must be added to the floors and connecting parts, so that noises of fireplace operation and cleaning will not carry over to neighboring apartments. When the firing unit is present, the base and the actual fireplace form are walled up, the fresh-air intake duct is connected, and the floor protection of non-flammable material is laid in front of the fireplace. Finally the mantelpiece, the formal heart of the fireplace, is installed or the decorative elements of the fireplace frame are attached. After the necessary drying time for all the masonry and plastered parts, the painter can finish the decorative work and the dust barrier can be removed—the work in the fireplace room is finished. What is necessarily stated here in the order of construction always requires a checking or coordinating control, so that the course of all the work is followed without problems, no mistakes are made, and the agreed-on schedule is kept. The larger the building task, the more showy the form and the more costly the materials to be used in the fireplace itself and the adjoining floor, wall, and ceiling area, the higher the cost naturally is, and the more meaningful it is to spend a certain amount of money on planning and supervision, so that in the end the fireplace takes its rightful place in the intended architectural interior ambience.

OPERATING ADVICE

The open fire in the fireplace represents not only a nice feeling of comfort but also a certain potential danger. Therefore the lawmakers require in the "Law on Technical Means of Work" that the operator of a fireplace must inform himself as to its function and operating, and the fireplace builder is required to familiarize his client with the fireplace, so as to avoid heat or fire damage in the building and keep the emissions as low as possible. The instructions begin with putting a new fireplace into service, which depending on its structure and type, only reaches its usefulness after the final drying of the masonry—which can take several weeks—after burning a few small fires with very dry wood. Open fireplaces, according to the German Federal Emission Protection Requirements, may be operated only with air-dried natural firewood (see "Fuels" chapter), their length being no more than two-thirds the size of the fire pit, and their diameter not exceeding thirty to forty centimeters—smaller firewood provides a stronger fire with complete combustion and is thus friendlier to the environment. The burning of garbage, painted or impregnated wood scraps or shavings is basically forbidden for reasons of environmental pollution, and the neighbors will be thankful to receive as little as possible from the operation of a strange fireplace.

Before the lighting of a fire, the closing flaps for the air intake and smoke outflow must be opened. A small fire of paper and kindling soon promotes the draft, and only when the small wood burns sufficiently should pieces of firewood be put in, and always added to at the right time, so as to avoid smoldering and heavy smoke. The traditional fireplace fire with an open hearth may be conducted only with supervision because of the heightened danger of glowing embers falling out.

Spark curtains or metal drapes, which of course may not close the hearth opening entirely, reduce the danger of fire, and can also provide a decorative element. When the glow of the fire is finally extinguished, the closing parts should be closed so that the room does not needlessly have hot air pulled away into the chimney and ash dust stirred up.

If functional or formal changes to the actual fireplace structure should be undertaken at some time, these must be agreed on with the district master chimney sweep. For if he should perceive changes in his regular inspections, he has the right to shut down the fireplace or require improvement.

FUELS

WHAT WOODS ARE SUITABLE FOR THE FIREPLACE?

Whoever burns wood in his fireplace from time to time need not have a guilty conscience. In burning, to be sure, carbon dioxide is released, but in the process of photosynthesis it can be taken up in the same quantity by nature. This process still takes place when wood is not burned but rots in the forest. Unlike the use of fossil fuels, we do not intervene wrongly in this natural circulation as long as no more wood is burned than grows back. The use of wood as a fuel also has several advantages, about which we should think, such as when wood is burned in a heating fireplace with a high degree of effect of up to 80% and thus serves as an alternative to other heating systems. Wood contains neither sulfur nor heavy metals, such as are freed in the burning of fossil fuels. Wood is inexpensive and safe to transport. Even if stored improperly, it cannot cause environmental damage, and its occurrence in our areas is almost inexhaustible, since trees constantly grow back. Its environmental balance is positive, even in times when forests are dying. The use of scrap wood from the forest helps to save fossil fuels. Besides, firewood is a by-product of a woodland economy that is produced in forest management. The profit in this selling of wood generally pays for reforestation and thus forest management. When it is burned, wood scarcely leaves ashes, and the few ashes that occur can be used as valuable mineral fertilizer in the gardens or flowerpots. So that all these promising processes can really take place in the fireplace, though, it is important to follow several rules carefully in using wood as a fuel: Only natural wood with attached bark, or in pieces (such as leftovers from carpentry) with a maximum residual moisture of 20% should be used as firewood. Damper wood hinders combustion; wood gases cannot ignite and flow unburned out of the chimney as pollutants. Besides, wood with residual moisture of about 50% produces only half the heat of air-dried wood with 15 to 20% moisture—so good storage pays. Heating wood is best cut in the frost period between December and February and split before it is stored, so as to shorten the drying time. It must be stored and dried two or three years, protected from rain and humidity. Only then does it burn well without producing pollutants. Wood sold in the fuel trade has these qualities: whoever buys his wood from a forester should inquire about storage time and residual moisture. When stored, wood should always be well ventilated by wind. For example, it should not be stacked in damp conditions in a poorly ventilated cellar, for it would not dry out there, but decay and get moldy. The types of wood that are suitable for fireplace burning have a comparable heating value between 4 kWh (beech) and 4.5 kWh (pine) per kilogram.

To be sure, they have very different burning behavior. Therefore the most important type of wood can be described briefly in terms of their heating value and characteristic burning behavior (see table at right).

The prices of the various types of wood vary a great deal depending on their form when delivered, condition, and vendor. The most expensive are small packed-up quantities of beech that can be bought at gas stations or supermarkets. It is better and more economical to buy larger quantities from a fuel dealer, who stacks the wood properly at the prepared place if asked to. It is naturally better to buy the trunks or pieces directly from a forester or forest owner and cut it to length and split it oneself. The purchase price is then very low, and even if cutting and splitting makes work, one has the feeling that one has done something for the endangered forest and also has gained some independence in providing one's own energy—for many who heat with wood and think of the environment, it is an experience of closeness to nature that they would not want to miss.

WOOD TYPE	HEATING VALUE kW/kg	BURNING BEHAVIOR
Birch	4.3	Burns slowly, steadily, first with yellow flame, later with blue, with good smell, few sparks, burns reliably and glows long when properly stacked.
Beech	4.0	Burns slowly with light flame, but sometimes sparks heavily and loudly, has hot glow with light ash formation.
Oak	4.2	Ideal slow-burning wood with varying flames, pleasant smell. Glows hot and long with white ashes. Must be stored long and dried well before burning.
Ash	4.2	Burns orange, very evenly, with good heating value. Must be stored well or it sweats.
Fruit woods	4.1	Burn slowly with uneasy flame, sometimes Crackle loudly with flying sparks.
Conifers	4.4	Fir, spruce and pine make a good fire, burn quickly with lively flames. Conifers crackle and sparks fly strongly.

APPENDIX

ARCHITECTS and PHOTO CREDITS

A. D. U. K.
Freie Planungsgruppe
Neues Bauen GmbH
Augsburg
p. 117: photo, Archiv
Architekten

Prof. Peter Berten
Dipl.-Ing. Architekt BDA
Berlin
p. 118: photo, OZON

Bernhard Busch
Dipl.-Ing. Architekt
AGN, Architekten,
Ingenieure,
Generalplaner
Ibbenbueren, Waiblingen,
Halle/Saale
pp. 24, 25, 53, 115: photos: Eslage
& Voss, Mettingen

Prof. Ulrich Goersmeier
Dipl.-Ing. Architekt
Cologne
pp. 14-15, photos, Thomas
Riehle, Cologne

De Biasio & Scherrer
Dipl.-Ing. Architekten
Zuerich
pp. 38, 50, photos, Archiv
Architekt

Franz C. Demblin
Dipl.-Ing. Architekt
Vienna
p. 17, photo, Archiv Architekt

Prof. Wolfgang Doering
Dipl.-Ing. Architekt
Duesseldorf
p. 12, photo, Thomas Riehle, Cologne

Michael Dressler
Dipl.-Ing. Innenarchitekt
Dressler & Eckardt GmbH
Munich
p. 69: photo, Klaus-Reiner
Klebe, Munich

Mechthild Friedrich-
Schoenberger
Muensing-Ammerland
p. 119: photo, H. J. Willig,
Geuener + Jahr, Hamburg

Sonja Gasparin
Architektin MMAG
Villach
pp. 70, 71: photos,
H. Kohlmeier, Villach

Gatermann + Schossig und
Partner, Architekten BDA
Cologne
p. 11, photo, A. Bednorz,
Cologne

Prof. Werner Girsberger
Dipl.-Ing. Architekt
Augsburg
p. 39, photo, M. Paal,
Munich

Hans Haeusler
Dipl.-Ing. Architekt
Vienna
p. 52, photo, Archiv
Architekt

Alois Juraschek
Dipl.-Ing. Architekt BDA
Aschau
p. 116, photo, Archiv Architekt

Prof.-Dipl.-Ing. Architekt
Wolfgang Knoll
Stuttgart
p. 62, photo, Archiv Architekt

Rouli Lecatsa
Dipl.-Ing. Architekt
Hamburg
p. 20: photo, A. Kiefer,
Hamburg

Rolf Leinweber
Dipl.-Ing. Architekt
Berlin
p. 26: photo, Stefan
Koppelkam, Berlin;
p. 55: photo, J. A.
Gonzalez, Berlin

Mai Zil Kusen
Architektin
Luebeck
pp. 21, 22: photos,
B. Goeppner, Luebeck

Gert M. Mayr-Keber
Dipl.-Ing. Architekt
Vienna
pp. 49, 142, photos,
S. Mayr-Keber, Vienna

Heinz Peter
Dipl.-Ing. Innenarchitekt
Steinbach
p. 54, photo, Archiv
Architekt

Guenter Pfeifer
Architekten GPF
Loerrach
p. 38, photo, Hans H.
Muenchhalfen, Loerrach

Prof. Dipl.-Ing. H. Pfeifer
Dipl.-Ing. Ch. Ellermann
und Partner
Architekten und Stadtplaner BDA
Luedinghausen/Berlin
p. 1, photo, Archiv Architekten

Peter Preller
Innenarchitekt
Hamburg
pp. 30, 56, photos, Archiv Architekt

Prof. Bertold Rosewich
Dipl.-Ing. Architekt
Karlsruhe
p. 14, photo, Archiv
Architekt; pp. 40, 41, sculptor
Jakob Broder; photos, Archiv
Architekt, p. 50, photo, Archiv Architekt

Dolf Schnebli, Tobias Ammann
Flora Ruchat-Roncati
Architekten BSA + Partner AG
Zuerich
p. 39, photo, Archiv Architekten

Hans H. Seibold
Dipl.-Ing. Architekt BDA
Hamburg
p. 56, Archiv Architekt

Spengler Wiescholek
Freie Architektin
Hamburg
p. 28, photo, H. J. Willig,
Gruner + Jahr, Hamburg

Hinrich Storch, Walter Ehlers
Dipl.-Ing. Architekten BDA
Hannover
p. 33, photo, Archiv Architekt

DEALERS AND BUILDERS

Accent Kamine GmbH
Neue Weyerstrasse 2
50519 Cologne
p. 107

The Antique Fireplace
Warehouse, Buckingham
Antiques Ltd.
194-200 Battersea Park Road
GB-London SW 11 4ND
pp. 96, 97

Boley Exklusive Kamine GmbH
Oststrasse 58
40667 Meerbusch (Buederich)
p. 54

Leonardo Caminetti GmbH
Budapester Strasse 4
10787 Berlin
Milchstrasee 21
20148 Hamburg
Ottostrasse 11
80333 Munich
Jungholzstrasse 6
CH-8050 Zuerich-Oerlikon
pp. 86, 87, 88, 89, 137, 138

Th. Evers
Architectural Antiques
De Koumen 58
NL-6433 KD Koensbroek/Heerlen
pp. 94, 95, 108 above

Michaele Ferk
Antike Spiegel und Kanine
Bahnhofstrasse 21
82340 Feldafing/ Starnberger See

Hallidays
Fine Antiques Limited
Carved Pine Mantelpieces Ltd.
The Old College
Dorchester-on-Thames

GB-Wallingford Oxon
OX 10 7HL
pp. 82, 83, 84, 85

Matten GmbH
56479 Niederrossbach
pp. 116, 120, 121, 122,
123, 124, 125

Mylin Antiquitaeten
Gaadt 26
25980 Westerland/Sylt
Schuetzenstrasse 17
25980 Westerland/Sylt
C.-P. Hansen-Allee
25980 Keitum/Sylt
Dorfstrasse 223
25920 Risum-Lindholm
p. 112

Oellers Imex GmbH
Auf der Komm 1
52457 Aldenhoven
pp. 106, 107, 108 below
pp. 93, 100, 101, 102, 103, 104, 105

Willem Schermerhorn
Antike Open Harden
Korte Laakenstraat 22
NL-2011 ZD Haarlem
pp. 110, 111

Scholl Keramik GmbH
Kurpfalzstrasse 141
67435 Neustadt/Weinstrasse
pp. 26, 52, 66, 67

Johann Tuemmers
Stuckwerkstaetten
Ueckendorfer Strasse 66-70
45886 Gelsenkirchen
pp. 90, 91

Ingfried Wodke GmbH
Kacheloefen Kamine
Rittweg 55-57
72070 Tuebingen
p. 64

PHOTO CREDITS

G. v. Bassewitz, Gruner + Jahr, Hamburg
pp. 34, 35, 43

Reiner Blunck, Tuebingen, pp. 20 above,
28 below, 32, 36, 37, 48, 51

F. Busam, Mainz, Architekturphoto
p. 23

G. Giesel, Gruner + Jahr, Hamburg
p. 16

A. Ginsburg, Gruner + Jahr
p. 57

L. Guderian, Gruner + Jahr
Hamburg, p. 68 below

A. Kiefer, Hamburg
p. 20

W. Krueger, Gruner + Jahr, Hamburg,
pp. 127, 128 upper right, Center, 129 above

Keith Scott Morton, Conde
Nast Publications, London p. 81

R. Nuettgens, Gruner +Jahr,
Hamburg, p. 63

OZON, Gruner + Jahr, Hamburg
p. 118

Margret Paul, Munich
pp. 93, 100, 101, 102, 103, 104, 105

Ralph Richter, Arthitekturphoto
pp. 98, 99

Tomas Riehle
Cologne, pp. 12, 13

S. Rock, Agentur Photo Selection
Hilaneh von Kories GmbH, Berlin
p. 9

G. Rogers, Gruner + Jahr, p. 78

Ri. Stradtmann, Gruner +Jahr,
Hamburg p. 68 above

W. Waldron, Stock Image Production,
Paris, pp. 2-3 and dust jacket

Joachim Werle, Hamburg
pp. 42, 44, 45, 46, 74, 76

J. Willebrand, Gruner + Jahr,
Hamburg, p. 114 above

H. J. Willig, Gruner + Jahr, Hamburg,
pp. 6, 18, 19, 27, 28 above, 29, 47, 60,
113, 114 below, 119

M. Wimmer, Gruner + Jahr
Hamburg, pp. 128 left,
Lower right, 129 below

The illustration on pp. 2-3: Interesting contrast between simple worked stone plates that surround the hearth and natural full-wood profiles that form the fireplace mask as Baroque stylistics.

Die Deutsche Bibliothek—CIP Einheitsaufnahme
Kamine Aktuelle Entwuerfe—Traditionelle Formen
Holger Reiners. [publisher]

Lithos Karl Findl, Icking
Setup Filmsatz Schroeter, Munich
Printing and binding
First printed in Germany, 1995
ISBN 3-7667-1152-0

OTHER SCHIFFER TITLES

www.schifferbooks.com

Outdoor Kitchens & Fireplaces. Tina Skinner. Here is the largest collection of images of landscapes, outdoor kitchens, and fireplaces available on the market today, and with those gorgeous photos come hundreds of ideas. Live vicariously as you leaf through these pages, and make the dream come true in your backyard with some of the many inspirations found here.

| Size: 8 1/2" x 11" | 200-plus images | 112pp. |
| ISBN: 978-0-7643-2955-5 | soft cover | $19.95 |

Fireplace Accessories. Dona Z. Meilach. Over 400 ideas for unusual fireplace designs reflect historical styles from Renaissance to Post-Modern. Fire screens, hoods, doors, andirons, grates, tongs, pokers, shovels, brooms, and their stands emerge as significant decorative items in today's homes. You will marvel at the artistry, variety, and craftsmanship.

Size: 8 1/2" x 11"	362 color	256pp.
	& 55 b/w photos	
ISBN: 0-7643-1615-X	hard cover	$49.95

Step-by-step to a Classic Fireplace Mantel. Steve Penberthy with Gary Jones. Build a classic mantel from stock materials and moldings, and tools found in the most basic of workshops. From measurement to the finished product, the authors take the reader through the complete

process. Every step is illustrated with a color photograph and a concise instruction. In the back are photographs of many design variations that can be made using the same building techniques.

Size: 8 1/2" x 11"	200+ color photos	64pp.
	& line drawings	
ISBN: 0-88740-653-X	soft cover	$12.95

Constructing a Fireplace Mantel: Step-by-Step from Plywood and Stock Moldings. Steve Penberthy with Lawrence S. Welsh. A step-by-step guide for building a beautiful mantelpiece with a recessed face plate, paneled designs on the legs and face plate, and the possibility for an infinite number of variations. Using plywood and stock moldings, the reader is taken through every step of the process, with each action illustrated with a color photograph and a clear explanation. Beginning with the drawing, it proceeds with building the carcass and ends with the application of the moldings and a clear spray finish. This book should make it possible for any woodworker to create a beautiful mantel.

Size: 8 1/2" x 11"	330 color photos,	64pp.
	+ drawings and plans	
ISBN: 0-7643-2457-8	soft cover	$14.95

Schiffer books may be ordered from your local bookstore, or they may be ordered directly from the publisher by writing to:
Schiffer Publishing, Ltd.
4880 Lower Valley Rd.
Atglen, PA 19310
(610) 593-1777; Fax (610) 593-2002
E-mail: Info@schifferbooks.com

Please visit our web site catalog at **www.schifferbooks.com** or write for a free catalog. Please include $5.00 for shipping and handling for the first two books and $2.00 for each additional book.
Full-price orders over $150 are shipped free in the U.S.

Printed in China